Woof and Wag

Bringing Home a Dog

by Rebecca Fjelland Davis

illustrated by Andi Carter

Special thanks to our advisers for their expertise:

Sharon Hurley, D.V.M.
New Ulm (Minnesota) Regional
Veterinary Center

Terry Flaherty, Ph.D., Professor of English
Minnesota State University, Mankato

PICTURE WINDOW BOOKS
Minneapolis, Minnesota

Editor: Jill Kalz
Designer: Hilary Wacholz
Page Production: Michelle Biedscheid
Art Director: Nathan Gassman
Associate Managing Editor: Christianne Jones
The illustrations in this book were created with mixed media.
Photo Credit: Sajko/Shutterstock, 23

Picture Window Books
151 Good Counsel Drive
P.O. Box 669
Mankato, MN 56002-0669
877-845-8392
www.picturewindowbooks.com

Library of Congress Cataloging-in-Publication Data
Davis, Rebecca Fjelland.
Woof and wag : bringing home a dog / by
Rebecca Fjelland Davis ; illustrated by Andi Carter.
p. cm. – (Get a pet)
Includes index.
ISBN 978-1-4048-4868-9 (library binding)
1. Dogs—Juvenile literature. I. Carter, Andi, 1976- ill. II. Title.
SF426.5.D39 2009
636.7–dc22   2008006430

Table of Contents

A New Dog

Jada is getting a new dog today! What kind of dog will she pick? Will it be big or small? A puppy or an adult? A dog with long hair or short hair?

TIP
Having a dog can cost a lot of money. Dogs need food, trips to the veterinarian, medicine, grooming supplies, toys, and more.

Having a dog is a lot of fun, but it is also a lot of work. Is Jada ready?

Most Popular Purebred Dog Breeds
Labrador Retriever
Yorkshire Terrier
German Shepherd
Golden Retriever
Beagle

Choosing a Dog

Jada is getting her dog from an animal shelter. She wants an active dog. Her family lives in the country. There is a lot of room for a dog to play.

Jada watches all of the dogs carefully. She wants to pick a healthy one. A healthy dog has clean, shiny fur. It looks at the things going on around it. It has clear, bright eyes, and teeth that are mostly white.

Jada names her new dog Sadie.

TIP

Animal shelters, pet stores, and breeders aren't the only places that have dogs. Check the want ads in the newspaper. Talk to a vet. Your local pet store may have listings of dogs that need good homes.

Coming Home

Jada's new dog is home! But she is a little scared. Everything is new to her. Jada takes her dog for a short walk before going in the house. This gives her dog a chance to go to the bathroom first.

Dogs need exercise every day. Jada takes her dog for a walk before school and after supper. She plays with her dog and lets her run in the fenced yard.

TIP

Dog training can teach you and your dog how to get along best with each other. It can also help your dog learn how to behave around other people and animals.

Time to Eat

Jada asks a vet what kind of food to feed her dog, how much to feed her, and how often. She makes sure her dog always has fresh water. Jada cleans the food and water bowls every few days.

Dogs like treats once in a while. Dog biscuits are best. Jada's dog never gets table scraps. They might make her sick.

TIP
Dog treats are usually high in fat, so don't give your dog too many. She may become overweight.

Grooming

All dogs need to be groomed. Jada brushes her short-haired dog about once a week. Long-haired dogs need brushing every day. Brushing helps to keep a dog's hair clean and smooth. Jada uses a firm bristle brush she bought at the pet store.

TIP

Many pet stores and vet clinics have groomers. For a fee, groomers will wash your dog, give her a haircut, and trim her claws.

When Jada's dog gets dirty, it's time for a bath. Jada uses a special dog shampoo and warm water. She is careful not to get soap in her dog's eyes or water in her dog's ears.

Keeping Clean

Jada takes her dog outside to go to the bathroom. They go to the same spot first thing in the morning, after meals, after playtime and naps, and before bedtime. Soon Sadie learns to whine or stand at the door when she needs to go to the bathroom.

TIP
Bring along a plastic bag when you and your dog go for a walk. Use it to pick up your dog's waste.

Every day, Jada scoops up her dog's waste. She seals it in a plastic bag and puts it in the garbage can.

Staying Healthy

Dogs need to go to the doctor just like people do. Jada takes her dog to a vet for a checkup soon after she gets her. The vet answers Jada's questions. He gives Jada's dog a few shots to keep her healthy.

Jada keeps her dog healthy at home, too. Chew toys help clean her dog's teeth. Mom makes sure Jada's dog gets medicine once a month. The medicine protects against fleas, heartworms, and other parasites.

TIP

State and local laws require rabies shots. Rabies is a disease spread through animal bites. Most states require a dog to wear a tag on her collar that says she has been protected against rabies.

Good Night, Dog!

Jada's dog sleeps in a crate at night. The crate is away from doors and windows that could let in cold air. Jada makes the crate cozy with a couple blankets.

Jada puts her dog to bed at about the same time each night. She gets her dog up at about the same time each morning, too.

TIP
If your new puppy cries at night, wrap a wind-up clock in a blanket near her. The ticking sounds like a heartbeat. It can make your puppy feel less lonely.

20

A Happy Pet

More than anything, dogs need love! Jada loves her dog and makes sure she is happy and healthy. With good care, Jada will have her tail-wagging friend for a long, long time.

Dog Close-up

A dog's **EYES** are on the front of its head.

A dog can move its **EARS** to locate sound better. Dog ears can hear many sounds that human ears cannot.

A dog's **NOSE** is usually black or brown, depending on the breed.

A dog uses its **TAIL** to communicate, or talk, with people and other dogs.

Because it doesn't sweat the way humans do, a dog cools off through its **MOUTH**. It pants, or breathes quickly.

A dog's feet are called **PAWS**.

Dog Life Cycle

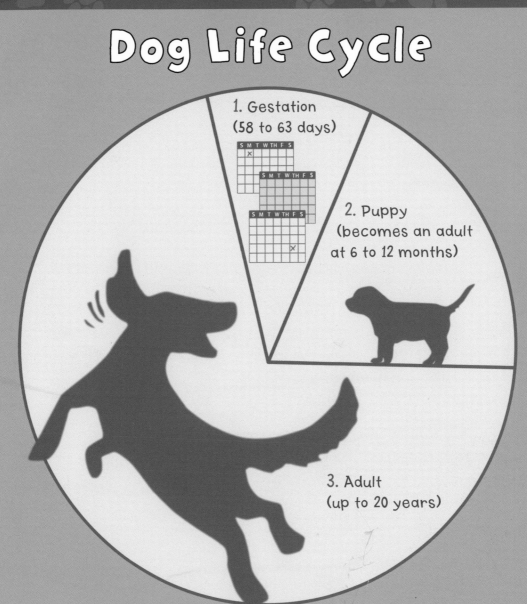

1. Gestation
(58 to 63 days)

2. Puppy
(becomes an adult
at 6 to 12 months)

3. Adult
(up to 20 years)

Glossary

animal shelter—a safe place where lost or homeless pets can stay

breed—a kind or type

breeder—a person who raises animals to sell

crate—a cage

fleas—tiny bloodsucking insects

gestation—the amount of time an unborn animal spends inside its mother

grooming—cleaning and making an animal look neat

parasites—animals or plants that live on other animals or plants

purebred—having parents of the same breed

veterinarian—a doctor who takes care of animals; vet, for short

Golden Retriever

To Learn More

More Books to Read

Dennis-Bryan, Kim. *Puppy Care: A Guide to Loving and Nurturing Your Pet.* New York: DK Pub., 2004.

Jeffrey, Laura S. *Dogs: How to Choose and Care for a Dog.* Berkeley Heights, N.J.: Enslow Publishers, 2004.

Landau, Elaine. *Your Pet Dog.* New York: Children's Press, 2007.

Preszler, June. *Caring for Your Dog.* Mankato, Minn.: Capstone Press, 2007.

On the Web

FactHound offers a safe, fun way to find Web sites related to topics in this book. All of the sites on FactHound have been researched by our staff.

1. Visit *www.facthound.com*
2. Type in this special code: 1404848681
3. Click on the FETCH IT button.

Your trusty FactHound will fetch the best sites for you!

Index

Look for all of the books in the Get a Pet series:

Flutter and Float: Bringing Home Goldfish
Purr and Pounce: Bringing Home a Cat
Scurry and Squeak: Bringing Home a Guinea Pig
Skitter and Scoot: Bringing Home a Hamster
Twitter and Tweet: Bringing Home a Bird
Woof and Wag: Bringing Home a Dog